太极导引杖（中英双语）

Taiji Daoyinzhang (Chinese-English)

孙佐枫 著 林记明 译

中国传统文化『走出去』丛书之二
Chinese Traditional Culture "Going Out" Series II

林记明 孙佐枫 丛书主编

河北出版传媒集团
河北人民出版社
石家庄

图书在版编目（CIP）数据

太极导引杖 : 汉、英 / 孙佐枫著 ; 林记明译. --
石家庄 : 河北人民出版社, 2023.12
（中国传统文化“走出去”丛书 / 林记明, 孙佐枫主编. 之二）
ISBN 978-7-202-16223-1

Ⅰ. ①太… Ⅱ. ①孙… ②林… Ⅲ. ①太极拳－基本知识－汉、英 Ⅳ. ①G852.11

中国国家版本馆CIP数据核字(2023)第000851号

丛 书 名	**中国传统文化“走出去”丛书之二** ZHONGGUO CHUANTONG WENHUA ZOUCHUQU CONGSHU ZHIER
丛书主编	林记明　孙佐枫
书　　名	**太极导引杖（汉英双语）** TAIJI DAOYINZHANG
著　　者	孙佐枫
译　　者	林记明
总 策 划	王斌贤
策划编辑	路殿国　李成轩
责任编辑	赵　蕊
美术编辑	王　婧
责任校对	余尚敏
摄　　影	蔡欣然
出版发行	河北出版传媒集团　河北人民出版社 （石家庄市友谊北大街 330 号）
印　　刷	河北新华第一印刷有限责任公司
开　　本	787 毫米×1092 毫米　1/16
印　　张	7
字　　数	96 000
版　　次	2023 年 12 月第 1 版　2023 年 12 月第 1 次印刷
书　　号	ISBN 978-7-202-16223-1
定　　价	29.00 元

<<< 前言

Foreword

杖，泛指棍棒，是人类最早使用的工具之一。在我国传统养生文化中，以杖作为器械进行身体锻炼的历史非常久远。现存最早文献史料记载见于1974年湖南长沙马王堆三号汉墓出土的《导引图》，其中有两幅手持长杖做出不同姿势的图像，这是目前所知运用杖来导引肢体进行养生锻炼的最早资料。用“杖”导引肢体的形式，表明了历史上曾出现的一种利用器械辅助导引的太极功法。

Zhang, which generally refers to stick, staff, cane or club in English, is one of the earliest instruments used by human beings. In the traditional health-preserving culture, Chinese people took *Zhang* as an instrument for physical exercise long ago. The earliest existing historical record is found in the *Daoyin Picture* unearthed from the No.3 Han Tomb in Mawangdui, Changsha City, Hunan Province in 1974, in which two figures of holding a long staff in different postures are the earliest known use of *Zhang* to guide the body's movements for health exercise. This practice with a staff shows that there existed a method of using an instrument to assist *Daoyin* in Chinese history.

太极导引杖取意“太极”阴阳和合、天人合一、内外相谐等传统文化理念，借鉴《导引图》中持杖图像及“以丈（杖）通阴阳”来表现功法特征，继承了传统持杖功法的精要，在与天地自然的交融中调和气息，平衡阴阳。集历史功法之精华，融入现代相关学科理论，以中西医、体育康复及相关科学理论为基础，具有明显的健身养生功效。整套功法动作以杖导引，圆转流畅，柔和缓慢，舒展连绵，动静相间，意境优美，意气相随。本书中英文对照，从功法操作、学练要领、功理功用和适宜症状等方面进行通俗易懂的论述。

Taiji Daoyinzhang adopts traditional Chinese Taiji concepts of balance between *Yin* and *Yang*, integration of man and nature, and harmony between inside and outside. By utilizing the concept of "connecting *Yin* and *Yang* with *Zhang*" and drawing inspirations from the figures of holding a staff in the *Daoyin Picture*, this skill inherits the essence of the traditional staff-holding exercises, where *Qi* and breathing are coordinated and *Yin* and *Yang* are balanced in the blend with nature. Taiji Daoyinzhang integrates the essence of ancient exercises and modern theories of related disciplines. Based on the traditional Chinese and western medicines, physical rehabilitation and related scientific theories, Taiji Daoyinzhang has obvious fitness and health effects. The whole set of movements is guided by a staff, flowing smoothly, circularly, softly and continuously, alternating between stillness and motion, with an artistic conception. This book in Chinese and English contains instructions, key points, functions and effects, and indications, which are easy to understand.

太极导引杖是一套简单易学易练，易于推广普及，针对性较强的健身方法，长期坚持练习，可改善人体的颈椎、胸椎、腰椎关节不适，预防跌倒摔跤，提高人体平衡能力，对心血管病、高血压、糖尿病、肺病、抑郁症等有不同程度的缓解改善作用，非常适宜在中外健身人群中普及推广。在倡导文化自信，建设文化强国和健康中国的时代背景下，本书对中国传统文化的国际传播具有文化和健身方面的重要价值。

Taiji Daoyinzhang is a highly targeted set of easy-to-learn and easy-to-practice health preservation exercise. Long term practice of this exercise can alleviate the discomfort of cervical, thoracic and lumbar joints, cardiovascular disorders, hypertension, diabetes, lung disease and depression, improve the balance of human body, and prevent falls. Therefore, it is very suitable for Chinese and foreign fitness enthusiasts. In the context of advocating cultural confidence and building a strong cultural and healthy China, this book is of great cultural and health value to the international dissemination of traditional Chinese culture.

器械介绍

About the Staff

杖可用白蜡杆、松木、硬杂木、竹子、藤木等多种材质制成，粗细均匀，表面光洁，也可以雕刻吉祥图案及养生文字。器械规格可根据身高和手掌大小及持握感觉确定，其长 105—125 厘米，直径 2.3—2.8 厘米。

The staff, which is used to refer to *Zhang* in this book, can be made of white ash, pine, hardwood, bamboo or rattan, with uniform thickness and smooth surface, and can also be carved with auspicious patterns and words about health preservation. The specifications of the staff can be determined according to the height of the practitioner, his or her palm size and the sensation of holding. It is often 105−125 centimetres long and 2.3−2.8 centimetres in diameter.

<<< 目录
Contents

预备势

Preparation

一、功法操作

I. Instructions

动作一：两脚并拢，自然站立；两肩松展，左手持杖，食指伸直贴于杖上，其余四指自然环握杖的下 1/3 处，两臂自然垂于体侧；目视前方。（图 1）（图 2 持杖）

Movement 1: Stand naturally with your feet together. With the shoulders relaxed and spread, hold the staff in a ring with your left hand about one third of its length from the lower end, the index finger straight against the staff. Both arms naturally hang down on both sides

图 1/Figure 1

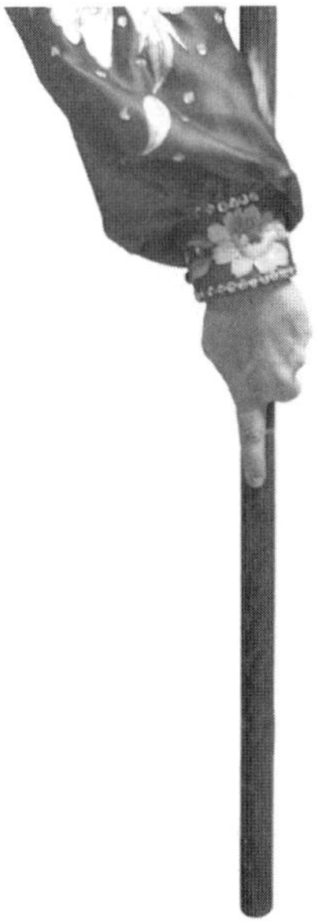

图 2 持杖 /Figure 2 hold the staff

of your body. Eyes look ahead. (Figure 1) (Figure 2 hold the staff)

动作二：左脚向左侧开步，约与肩同宽，两脚尖向前；左手持杖的下端向内抬起，右手于腹前接握杖，左手滑杖，两手水平环握杖与肩同宽，握杖时掌心虚空，拇指自然压于食指第一指节，两臂自然垂落；目视前方。（图 3）（图 4 环握杖）

Movement 2: Take a step to the left with your left foot, the feet shoulder-width apart, toes pointing forward. Lift the lower end of the staff inward with your left hand, your right hand takes the staff in front of the abdomen. Slide your left hand on the staff to the left so that both of your hands horizontally hold the staff in a ring with the same width as the shoulder, palms hollow and thumbs naturally pressed on the first knuckles of the index fingers. Both of your arms naturally hang down. Eyes look ahead. (Figure 3) (Figure 4 hold the staff in a ring)

图 3/Figure 3

图 4 环握杖 /Figure 4 hold the staff in a ring

动作三：躯干动作保持不变，两手环握杖轻贴腹部，手腕向内卷曲，卷杖上提轻轻摩运至两乳下；目视前方。（图 5）

Movement 3: With the position of your torso unchanged, hold the staff in a ring with your hands and rub it up against the abdomen to under the breasts, wrists flexed inward. Eyes look ahead. (Figure 5)

动作四：躯干动作保持不变，两手环握杖手腕放松，向下沿腹部摩运至两臂自然伸展；目视前方。（图 6）

Movement 4: With the position of your torso unchanged, hold the staff in a ring with your hand and rub it down along the abdomen, wrists relaxed, until your arms naturally extend. Eyes look ahead. (Figure 6)

动作五：同动作三。（图 7）

Movement 5: Repeat Movement 3. (Figure 7)

动作六：同动作四。（图 8）

Movement 6: Repeat Movement 4. (Figure 8)

本势动作杖向上、向下摩运为 1 遍，共做 3 遍。

Rubbing the staff up and down form a round. Do three rounds.

图 5/Figure 5

图 6/Figure 6

图 7/Figure 7

图 8/Figure 8

二、学练要领

II. Key Points

1. 并步站立时，百会穴虚领，下颏微收，周身中正，唇齿合拢，自然呼吸，内心平静。

When standing with feet together, keep your body upright, pull up *Baihui* acupoint, tuck in the chin slightly, breathe naturally, and calm your mind, lips and teeth closed.

2. 卷杖上提时，卷腕、屈肘、上提要依次连贯，配合吸气完成；向下松腕、伸臂、落杖依次连贯，配合呼气完成。

When rubbing the staff upward, it is imperative to flex your wrists, bend your elbows and raise the staff in sequence with inhalation. When rubbing the staff downward, it is imperative to relax your wrists, extend your elbows and drop the staff in sequence with exhalation.

3. 完成动作时，身体从始至终保持中正安舒的状态。

In the process, keep your body upright, calm and easy.

三、功理功用

III. Functions and Effects

1. 杖上、下摩运时，以杖导引动作，可以导引清气上行，浊气下降，调理身心，体松心静，使习练者逐步进入练功状态。

When rubbing the staff upward or downward, use the staff to guide the movements, which can guide the clear *Qi* to go up and the turbid *Qi* down to relax the body and calm the mind so that you gradually enter the state of practicing Taiji Daoyinzhang.

2. 动作、呼吸、意念协调配合，心神宁静，气沉丹田，内安脏腑，外松筋骨，有利于气血运行。

Coordinate the movements, breathing and mental activities. Calm your mind and sink *Qi* to *Dantian* to nurture internal organs and relax bones and muscles, which is beneficial to the circulation of *Qi* and blood.

四、适宜症状

IV. Indications

1. 可以缓解精神紧张、焦虑、神经衰弱等相关症状。

It can relieve mental stress, anxiety and neurasthenia.

2. 改善练习者血液循环，起到温煦手足的作用。

It can improve the blood circulation, warming your hands and feet.

第一式　艄公摇橹

Posture 1　Boatman Paddles

一、功法操作

I. Instructions

动作一：接预备势，两腿屈膝下蹲，左腿向左斜前方上步，脚跟着地，脚尖勾起；两手腕向内卷曲，卷杖上提轻轻摩运至两乳下，然后翻腕屈肘；目视前方。（图 9 正面、图 9 侧面）

Movement 1: Continuing from the end of the Preparation, bend your knees and step forward to the left with your left foot, heel on the ground and toes up. With your wrists flexed inward, rub the staff up gently with your hands to under the breasts. With your wrists flexed outward, bend your elbows. Eyes look ahead. (Figure 9 front, Figure 9 side)

图 9 正面 /Figure 9 front

图 9 侧面 /Figure 9 side

动作二：动作不停，左脚脚掌落地，重心前移成左弓步，同时两掌自然舒展，用虎口夹持杖，向上。向前弧形摇杖至与肩同高；目视前方。（图 10 正面、图 10 侧面）（图 11 夹持杖）

Movement 2: Without a pause, the ball of the left foot lands on the ground, and the weight shifts forward into a left-weighted bow stance. At the same time, the palms naturally extend to clamp the staff in *Hukou*. Row the staff up to the front in an arc to shoulder height. Eyes look ahead. (Figure 10 front, Figure 10 side) (Figure 11 clamp the staff)

图 10 正面 /Figure 10 front

图 10 侧面 /Figure 10 side

图 11 夹持杖 /Figure 11 clamp the staff

动作三：动作不停，弓步动作保持不变，两掌继续夹持杖弧形下落摇杖至与腰同高；目视杖的方向。（图 12 正面、图 12 侧面）

Movement 3: Without a pause, keep the left-weighted bow stance. Your hands continue to clamp the staff and row it down to waist height. Eyes follow the direction of the staff. (Figure 12 front, Figure 12 side)

图 12 正面 /Figure 12 front

图 12 侧面 /Figure 12 side

动作四：重心后移，右腿屈膝，松胯后坐，左腿自然伸展，脚尖向上勾起，脚跟着地，同时两手环握杖自然垂落于腹前，杖轻贴下腹部，同时身体转向右斜前方；目视右前方。（图 13 正面、图 13 侧面）

Movement 4: With the weight shifting backward, bend your right knee. Relax your hips and sit backward. Straighten your left leg naturally, toes up and heel on the ground. At the same time, your hands hold the staff in a ring and bring it down to touch your abdomen gently. Turn your body to the right front. Eyes look ahead to the right. (Figure 13 front, Figure 13 side)

图 13 正面 /Figure 13 front

图 13 侧面 /Figure 13 side

动作五：下肢动作保持不变。身体向左转至正前方，同时两手环握杖，腕向内卷曲，卷杖上提轻轻摩运至两乳下，然后翻腕屈肘；目视前方。（图 14）

Movement 5: With the position of your legs unchanged, turn your body to the left, the torso facing the straight forward. At the same time, with the wrists flexed inward, hold the staff in a ring with your hands and lift it, gently rubbing it to under your breasts. Flex your wrist outward and bend your elbows. Eyes look ahead. (Figure 14)

动作六：同动作二。（图 15）

Movement 6: Repeat Movement 2. (Figure 15)

动作七：同动作三。（图 16）

Movement 7: Repeat Movement 3. (Figure 16)

动作八：同动作四。（图 17）

Movement 8: Repeat Movement 4. (Figure 17)

图 14/Figure 14

图 15/Figure 15

图 16/Figure 16

图 17/Figure 17

动作九：同动作五。（图 18）

Movement 9: Repeat Movement 5. (Figure 18)

动作十：左脚收回，两腿由屈到伸成并步站立，同时两掌自然舒展，用虎口夹持杖，向上，向前弧形摇杖至与肩同高；目视前方。（图 19）

Movement 10: Bring your left foot back to the right one. Straighten your legs and stand with feet together. At the same time, extend your palms naturally, clamping the staff in *Hukou* and rowing it upward and forward to shoulder height. Eyes look ahead. (Figure 19)

图 18/Figure 18

图 19/Figure 19

动作十一：动作不停，并步站立动作保持不变，两掌继续夹持杖弧形下落摇杖画圆垂落至腹前。（图 20）

Movement 11: Without a pause, stand with feet together. Your two hands continue to clamp the staff and row it down to the front of the abdomen. (Figure 20)

动作十二：同动作一，唯左右相反。（图 21）

Movement 12: Repeat Movement 1, but with left and right reversed. (Figure 21)

图 20/Figure 20

图 21/Figure 21

动作十三：同动作二，唯左右相反。（图 22）

Movement 13: Repeat Movement 2, but with left and right reversed. (Figure 22)

动作十四：同动作三，唯左右相反。（图 23）

Movement 14: Repeat Movement 3, but with left and right reversed. (Figure 23)

动作十五：同动作四，唯左右相反。（图 24）

Movement 15: Repeat Movement 4, but with left and right reversed. (Figure 24)

动作十六：同动作五，唯左右相反。（图 25）

Movement 16: Repeat Movement 5, but with left and right reversed. (Figure 25)

动作十七：同动作十，唯左右相反。（图 26）

Movement 17: Repeat Movement 10, but with left and right reversed. (Figure 26)

动作十八：同动作十一。（图 27）

Movement 18: Repeat Movement 11. (Figure 27)

图 22/Figure 22

图 23/Figure 23

图 24/Figure 24

图 25/Figure 25

图 26/Figure 26

图 27/Figure 27

本式动作左前方摇杖、右前方摇杖各做 3 遍。

Row the staff to the left front three times and then to the right front three times.

二、学练要领

II. Key Points

1. 弓步时，两脚不要在一条直线上，步幅大小、高低因人而异，舒适自然，保持身体平衡状态。

When in bow stance, both feet should not be in a straight line. The size and height of the stance varies from person to person. Be comfortable and natural. Keep your body in a balanced state.

2. 摇杖时，肘关节保持自然微屈，沉肩、坠肘、松腕，节节贯穿，幅度在肩、腰之间画圆。

When rowing the staff, keep your elbows bent and dropping, shoulders sinking, and wrists relaxed, moving the joints in sequence.

In the range of drawing circles, the staff is no higher than the shoulder and no lower than the waist.

3. 完成动作时，始终保持上下肢配合协调，柔和流畅，百会虚领，呼吸自然。

In the process, always keep the upper and lower limbs coordinated, gentle and smooth. Pull up *Baihui* acupoint, and breathe naturally.

三、功理功用

III. Functions and Effects

1. 腕关节的有节律的屈伸运动，可以有效按摩腕部原穴，对手少阴心经、手厥阴心包经、手太阴肺经有一定的刺激疏导作用，可以起到养心安神的作用。

The rhythmic flexion and extension of the wrists can effectively massage the acupoints on the wrists to stimulate and dredge the Heart Meridian of Hand-*Shaoyin*, Pericardium Meridian of Hand-*Jueyin* and Lung Meridian of Hand-*Taiyin*, nourishing the heart and soothing the nerves.

2. 弓步下蹲时，可加强股四头肌、小腿后侧肌群等肌肉收缩，能有效增强下肢力量，提高身体稳定性，促进血液循环。

The bow stance can effectively strengthen quadriceps and posterior calf muscle groups to improve the stability of your body and promote the circulation of blood.

四、适宜症状

IV. Indications

1. 对冠心病、心绞痛、心慌、失眠、健忘、肋间神经痛等有一定的缓解作用。

It is effective in relieving coronary heart disease, angina pectoris, panic attacks, insomnia, forgetfulness and intercostal neuralgia.

2. 有利于缓解腕部肌肉劳损疼痛等症状。

It is conducive to the relief of wrist muscle strain and pain.

3. 重心前后移动，活动髋关节，可有效预防股骨头坏死。

Shifting the weight forward or backward and moving the hip joints can effectively prevent necrosis of the femoral head.

第二式　轻舟缓行

Posture 2　Boat Progresses Leisurely

一、功法操作

I. Instructions

动作一：接上式，两腿屈膝下蹲，左脚向前上一步，脚跟着地，脚尖勾起；随之腰向右转，两膝保持正前方，同时，两手环握杖，由身体右侧，经后下方向上画圆弧，举至头右侧上方；目视前方。（图 28 正面、图 28 侧面）

Movement 1: Continuing from the end of the previous posture, bend your knees, and step forward with your left foot, heel on the ground and toes up. Then turn your waist to the right, knees straight

图 28 正面 /Figure 28 front

图 28 侧面 /Figure 28 side

ahead. At the same time, hold the staff in a ring with your hands and draw an arc from the right side of your body, through the back rear to the upper right, above your head. Eyes look ahead. (Figure 28 front, Figure 28 side)

动作二：身体动作保持不变，右手指舒展，掌心向上成托杖；目视前方。（图 29）

Movement 2: With the position of your body unchanged. Extend the fingers of your right hand, holding the staff with the palm up. Eyes look ahead. (Figure 29)

图 29/Figure 29

动作三：动作不停，右手腕外旋约 180° 环握杖，随即重心前移，两膝自然伸展，左脚踏实，右脚尖点地，身体左转约 45°，杖从上向前、向下，经身体左侧向后下方画圆弧，右手至左腰侧，左手至身后左斜下方；目视前方。（图 30 正面、图 30 侧面）

Movement 3: Without a pause, rotate your right wrist about 180 degrees outward to hold the staff in a ring, then shift the weight forward, knees naturally extended, the left foot firmly planted on the ground, the toes of the right foot on the ground. Turn your body about 45 degrees to the left. The staff draws an arc from above forward, downward, via the left side of the body, to the lower rear, your right hand at the left waist and your left hand at the lower left rear. Eyes look ahead. (Figure 30 front, Figure 30 side)

图 30 正面 /Figure 30 front

图 30 侧面 /Figure 30 side

动作四：重心后移，右腿屈膝，左腿膝关节稍弯曲，两脚尖向前，同时杖从身体左侧向后、向上画弧，举至头左侧上方。（图 31 正面、图 31 侧面）

Movement 4: With the weight shifting backward, bend your right leg, your left knee slightly bent, and the toes of your feet forward. At the same time, the staff draws an arc backward and upward from the left side of the body to the upper left of your head. (Figure 31 front, Figure 31 side)

图 31 正面 /Figure 31 front

图 31 侧面 /Figure 31 side

动作五：身体动作保持不变，右手指舒展，掌心向上成托杖；目视前方。（图 32）

Movement 5: With the position of your body unchanged. Extend the fingers of your right hand, holding the staff with the palm up. Eyes look ahead. (Figure 32)

动作六：手腕内旋约 180° 环握杖，随即左脚经右踝内侧向后退一步，左腿屈膝，右腿膝关节稍弯曲，右脚跟着地，脚尖向上勾起，杖从上向前、向下，经身体右侧向后下方画圆弧，左手至右腰侧，右手至身后右斜下方；目视前方。（图 33 正面、图 33 侧面）

Movement 6: Rotate your right wrist about 180 degrees inward to hold the staff in a ring, then take a step backward with your left foot from inside your right ankle. Bend your left leg with your right knee slightly bent, your right heel on the ground and right toes up. The staff draws an arc from above, forward, downward, via the right side of the body, to the lower rear, your left hand at the right waist and your right hand at the lower right rear. Eyes look ahead. (Figure 33 front, Figure 33 side)

图 32/Figure 32

图 33 正面 /Figure 33 front

图 33 侧面 /Figure 33 side

动作七：右脚踏实，左脚向前上步，与右脚并拢，屈膝半蹲，同时杖继续由身体右侧向后、向上画圆弧，举至头右上方。（图34 正面、图 34 侧面）

Movement 7: With the right foot firmly planted, bring your left foot forward to stand together with your right foot, knees bent in a half squat. At the same time, the staff continues to draw an arc backward and upward from the right side of your body to the upper right of your head. (Figure 34 front, Figure 34 side)

图 34 正面 /Figure 34 front

图 34 侧面 /Figure 34 side

动作八：两腿自然站立，杖从上向前、向下，经身体左侧向后下方画圆弧，右手至左腰侧，左手至身后右斜下方；目视前方。（图 35 正面、图 35 侧面）

Movement 8: Straighten your legs. The staff draws an arc from above, forward, downward, via the left side of the body, to the lower rear, your right hand at the left waist and your left hand at the lower right rear. Eyes look ahead. (Figure 35 front, Figure 35 side)

图 35 正面 /Figure 35 front

图 35 侧面 /Figure 35 side

动作九：同动作一，唯左右相反。（图 36）

Movement 9: Repeat Movement 1, but with left and right reversed. (Figure 36)

动作十：同动作二，唯左右相反。（图 37）

Movement 10: Repeat Movement 2, but with left and right reversed. (Figure 37)

动作十一：同动作三，唯左右相反。（图 38）

Movement 11: Repeat Movement 3, but with left and right reversed. (Figure 38)

动作十二：同动作四，唯左右相反。（图 39）

Movement 12: Repeat Movement 4, but with left and right reversed. (Figure 39)

动作十三：同动作五，唯左右相反。（图 40）

Movement 13: Repeat Movement 5, but with left and right reversed. (Figure 40)

动作十四：同动作六，唯左右相反。（图 41）

Movement 14: Repeat Movement 6, but with left and right reversed. (Figure 41)

图 36/Figure 36

图 37/Figure 37

图 38/Figure 38

图 39/Figure 39

图 40/Figure 40

图 41/Figure 41

动作十五：同动作七，唯左右相反。（图 42）

Movement 15: Repeat Movement 7, but with left and right reversed. (Figure 42)

图 42/Figure 42

动作十六：同动作八，唯左右相反。（图 43）

Movement 16: Repeat Movement 8, but with left and right reversed. (Figure 43)

图 43/Figure 43

本式一左一右为 1 遍，共做 2 遍。

The movements on the left and the movements on the right form a round. Do two rounds.

二、学练要领

II. Key Points

1. 杖在体侧画弧时，要连绵不断，上下连贯，以腰的左右转动来带动杖的圆弧动作。

When the staff draws an arc on the side of the body, it should be continuous, with the waist turning left or right to drive the staff's circular motion.

2. 向前上步或向后退步时，两脚内侧应在一条直线上，两脚尖正向前。

When stepping forward or backward, the insides of both feet should be in a straight line, toes pointing forward.

3. 呼吸配合遵循起吸落呼的原则，杖起吸气，杖落呼气。

When breathing, you should follow the principle of inhaling as the staff rises and exhaling as the staff falls.

三、功理功用

III. Functions and Effects

1. 杖在体侧画弧，突出了手腕的旋转和肩部的圆转运动，畅通了手三阴、手三阳经脉，强心益肺，通调三焦，润肠化结。

The staff draws an arc on the side of the body, which emphasizes the rotation of the wrists and the circular movement of the shoulders, unblocking the three *Yang* and *Yin* meridians of the hands. It helps to strengthen the heart, benefit the lungs, regulate the tri-energizer, and moisten the intestines and dissolve the knots.

2. 以腰的左右转动来带动杖的圆弧动作，有助于调理肩背腰部肌肉，松解其粘连，缓解其疼痛。

The left or right turn of the waist drives the circular movement of the staff, which helps to condition the shoulders, back and lumbar muscles, release their adhesions and relieve their pain.

3. 踝关节的屈伸运动可以加强对足三阴、足三阳经脉的刺激，有利于疏肝利胆，通调膀胱。

The flexion and extension of the ankle can enhance the stimulation of three *Yang* and *Yin* meridians of the foot, which is conducive to detoxifying the liver and gallbladder, and regulating the bladder.

四、适宜症状

IV. Indications

1. 预防和缓解胃胀、胃疼、胃下垂，消化不良，食欲不振，便秘，腹泻等症状。

It can prevent and relieve stomach bloating, stomach pain, gastroptosis, indigestion, loss of appetite, constipation and diarrhea.

2. 有利于缓解肩、肘、腕、颈、背、腰等部位的肌肉疼痛。

It can relieve muscle pain in the shoulders, elbows, wrists, neck, back and lumbar region.

第三式　风摆荷叶

Posture 3　Wind Swings Lotus Leaf

一、功法操作

I. Instructions

动作一：接上式，左脚侧开一步，约与肩同宽，脚尖向前，右腿稍屈膝，左腿自然伸展，两手环握杖卷腕，杖向右前方抬起，约与小腹同高；目视右前下方。（图 44）

Movement 1: Continuing from the end of the previous posture, take a step to the left with your left foot, about shoulder-width apart, toes forward. Bend your right leg slightly, and straighten your left leg naturally. Hold the staff in a ring with your hands and rotate your wrists, lifting it forward to the right, about the same height as the lower abdomen. Eyes look downward to the right. (Figure 44)

图 44/Figure 44

动作二：身体保持中正，两腿屈膝下蹲，两手由环握杖变为虎口夹持杖，手心向下，经腹前从右向左前方画平圆。（图 45）

Movement 2: With your body upright, bend your knees, change your hands from holding the staff in a ring to clamping the staff in *Hukou*, palms down, and draw a flat circle with the staff from the right to the left in front of your abdomen. (Figure 45)

动作三：两腿自然站立，两手环握杖卷腕，弧形收杖于腹左侧；目视左前下方。（图 46）

Movement 3: Straighten your legs naturally. Hold the staff in a ring with your hands and rotate your wrists to bring it in an arc to the left side of the abdomen. Eyes look down to the left front. (Figure 46)

图 45/Figure 45

图 46/Figure 46

动作四：两腿动作保持不变，身体右转，杖由左向右横向摩运小腹，右手引杖至右肩右后方，左手环握杖至右胁肋部。（图 47）

Movement 4: With the position of your legs unchanged, turn your body to the right. The staff rubs the abdomen horizontally from the left to the right. The right hand lifts the staff to the right rear of the right shoulder, and the left hand holds the staff in a ring and brings it to the right ribs. (Figure 47)

动作五：身体左转至正前方，同时左手稍向右上移动，至右胸前，右手从右向左画平圆至左胸前，右臂在上，左臂在下，屈肘叠臂于胸前，同时松胯屈膝半蹲，杖由右向左画平圆，水平放于胸前；目视前方。（图 48）

Movement 5: Turn your body left, facing forward. At the same time, the left hand moves slightly upward to the right chest, and the right hand draws a flat circle from the right to the left chest. With the right arm above and the left arm below, fold your arms in front of the chest. At the same time, relax the hips and bend the knees in a half squat, and draw a flat circle with the staff from the right to the left, ending in front of the chest. Eyes look ahead. (Figure 48)

图 47/Figure 47

图 48/Figure 48

动作六：两腿自然站立，左手握杖经腰前向身体左侧画平圆，与腰同高，左臂微屈，右手握杖上提至左手上方，右臂自然伸展，贴于右耳侧，上体成左侧屈，与地面约成 45° 夹角，杖立于身体左侧；目视杖的方向。（图 49）

Movement 6: Straighten your legs naturally. Hold the staff with your left hand and draw a flat circle across the front of the waist to the left side of the body, the same height as the waist, left arm slightly bent. Hold the staff with your right hand and lift it up to above the left hand, right arm naturally stretched out, touching the back of the right ear. The upper body bends to the left, forming an angle of 45 degrees with the ground, the staff vertical on the left side. Eyes look in the direction of the staff. (Figure 49)

动作七：身体动作保持不变，两手十指自然伸展夹持杖，稍停；目视杖的方向。（图 50）

Movement 7: With the position of your body unchanged, extend the ten fingers of your hands naturally to clamp the staff. Pause for a while. Eyes look in the direction of the staff. (Figure 50)

图 49/Figure 49

图 50/Figure 50

动作八：两腿不动，身体直立，仰头，杖由左侧向上弧形举至头上方，直腕，十指尖向上夹持杖，两臂自然伸展；目视上方。（图 51）

Movement 8: With the feet still, erect your body, head tilted up. Raise the staff in an upward arc from the left side to above the head, wrists straight, fingertips upward to clamp the staff, arms naturally extended. Eyes look upward. (Figure 51)

动作九：两腿屈膝下蹲，杖下落至胸前，随即从两乳下沿小腹方向，向下摩运至两臂自然垂落，两掌心向下；目视前方。（图 52）

Movement 9: Bend your knees. Lower the staff to the chest, and then rub it downward from under the two breasts to your abdomen. Both arms naturally hang down, palms facing downward. Eyes look ahead. (Figure 52)

图 51/Figure 51

图 52/Figure 52

动作十：左脚收回成并步站立，杖的位置保持不变；目视前方。（图 53）

Movement 10: Bring your left foot back and stand with your feet together, the position of the staff remaining the same. Eyes look ahead. (Figure 53)

动作十一：同动作一，唯左右相反。（图 54）

Movement 11: Repeat Movement 1, but with left and right reversed. (Figure 54)

图 53/Figure 53

图 54/Figure 54

动作十二：同动作二，唯左右相反。（图 55）

Movement 12: Repeat Movement 2, but with left and right reversed. (Figure 55)

动作十三：同动作三，唯左右相反。（图 56）

Movement 13: Repeat Movement 3, but with left and right reversed. (Figure 56)

动作十四：同动作四，唯左右相反。（图 57 正面、图 57 侧面）

Movement 14: Repeat Movement 4, but with left and right reversed. (Figure 57 front, Figure 57 side)

图 55/Figure 55

图 56/Figure 56

图 57 正面 /Figure 57 front

图 57 侧面 /Figure 57 side

动作十五：同动作五，唯左右相反。（图 58）

Movement 15: Repeat Movement 5, but with left and right reversed. (Figure 58)

动作十六：同动作六，唯左右相反。（图 59）

Movement 16: Repeat Movement 6, but with left and right reversed. (Figure 59)

图 58/Figure 58

图 59/Figure 59

动作十七：同动作七。（图 60）

Movement 17: Repeat Movement 7. (Figure 60)

动作十八：同动作八，唯左右相反。（图 61）

Movement 18: Repeat Movement 8, but with left and right reversed. (Figure 61)

动作十九：同动作九。（图 62）

Movement 19: Repeat Movement 9. (Figure 62)

动作二十：同动作十，唯左右相反。（图 63）

Movement 20: Repeat Movement 10, but with left and right reversed. (Figure 63)

图 60/Figure 60

图 61/Figure 61

图 62/Figure 62

图 63/Figure 63

本式一左一右为 1 遍，共做 2 遍。

The movements on the left and the movements on the right form a round. Do two rounds.

二、学练要领

II. Key Points

1. 两手环握杖向左右画圆时，要以腰的动作带动杖的水平圆转，两手运动要有主有从地引导杖完成动作。

When your hands hold the staff in a ring and draw a flat circle to the left or right, the staff should be driven by the waist, one hand primary, the other secondary.

2. 杖从左右两侧向上举时，眼睛要随杖环视，再目视上方，注意保持身体平衡。

When you raise the staff upward from the left or right side, your eyes should follow the staff and then look upward. Keep the body balanced.

三、功理功用

III. Functions and Effects

1. 身体侧屈，可以有效刺激胆经、冲脉和任督二脉等重要经脉，有助于疏肝利胆，平抑肝阳上亢，促进全身气血运行。

Lateral bending of the body can effectively stimulate the Gallbladder Meridian, the Thoroughfare Meridian, *Ren* Meridian and *Du* Meridian, which can help to soothe the liver and the gallbladder, calm the hyperactivity of liver *Yang*, and promote the circulation of *Qi* and blood throughout the body.

2. 根据整脊学实践及理论，脊柱左、右侧屈动作，可以预防或调理脊柱生理弯曲不对称、不平衡等现象，有效地避免脊柱在形态上的不良变化。

According to chiropractic theory and practice, bending of the spine to the left or right can prevent or regulate spinal asymmetry, effectively avoiding spinal deformity.

四、适宜症状
IV. Indications

可以缓解肝胆脏腑疾病、脾胃消化不良、泌尿系统疾病、颈椎病、腰肌劳损、脊柱侧弯、椎间盘突出等症状。

It can relieve symptoms such as hepatobiliary diseases, dyspepsia, urinary system diseases, cervical spondylosis, lumbar muscle strain, scoliosis, and disc herniation.

第四式　船夫背纤

Posture 4　Boatman Tows Boat

一、功法操作

I. Instructions

动作一：接上式，杖的位置保持不变；两腿屈膝，身体左转，左脚向左侧开一步，脚跟着地，脚尖勾起；目视左前方。（图 64）

Movement 1: Continuing from the end of the previous posture, with the position of the staff unchanged, bend your legs, and turn your body to the left. Take a step to the left with your left foot, heel on the ground, toes up. Eyes look to the left front. (Figure 64)

图 64/Figure 64

动作二：动作不停，左腿屈膝下蹲，右腿膝关节伸展成左弓步，同时，左手引杖端由腹前向左、向上画弧至头斜上方，右手

环握杖跟随左手运动路线至约与腰同高，杖由水平至接近垂直于地面；目视左前方。（图 65）

Movement 2: Without a pause, bend your left leg further and extend your right leg to form a left-weighted bow stance. At the same time, your left hand leads the end of the staff, drawing an arc from the front of the abdomen to the left, upward, and to the upper front of the head; your right hand grasps the staff in a ring and follows your left hand's movement to about the same height as the waist, the staff nearly vertical to the ground. Eyes look to the left front. (Figure 65)

图 65/Figure 65

动作三：动作不停，左弓步动作保持不变，左手向杖的左把端滑杖，继续环握杖向后、向下画弧至左腰侧，卷腕并摩运左胁肋部，右手环握杖继续向前、向上画弧至体前，约与胸同高；目视左前方。（图 66 正面、图 66 侧面）

Movement 3: Without a pause, keep the left-weighted bow stance unchanged. Slide your left hand on the staff toward its left end, and continue to hold the staff in a ring and draw an arc backward and downward to the left waist. Rotate your wrist and rub your left rib. Your right hand holds the staff in a ring and continues to draw an arc forward and upward to the front of your body at about chest height. Eyes look to the left front. (Figure 66 front, Figure 66 side)

图 66 正面 /Figure 66 front

图 66 侧面 /Figure 66 side

动作四：重心右移，右脚掌向外蹍转，左脚尖内扣，两脚尖正向前，两腿自然站立，同时，左手环握杖继续向下、向前轻贴左腿外侧，继续向上画弧至与肩同高，肘关节弯曲，右手向杖的右把端滑杖，继续环握杖从体后向上、向右、向下画弧与肩同高，肘关节弯曲，杖放于肩上，与地面平行；目视前方。（图 67）

Movement 4: With the weight shifting to the right, turn your right foot outward and your left foot inward to stand naturally, toes pointing forward. At the same time, your left hand holds the staff in a ring and continues to draw an arc downward, forward, touching the outside of your left leg, and upward to the same height as the shoulder, elbow bent. Slide your right hand on the staff toward its right end and continue to hold the staff in a ring and draw an arc from behind your body upward, to the right and downward to the same height as the shoulder, elbow bent. The staff is placed on the shoulder, parallel to the ground. Eyes look ahead. (Figure 67)

图 67/Figure 67

动作五：右脚尖外展约 90°，身体稍右转，两手环握杖在肩上继续向右摩运；目视右前方。（图 68）

Movement 5: With your right toes turning outward by about 90 degrees, your body turns slightly to the right. Your hands hold the staff in a ring and continue to rub it to the right on your shoulders. Eyes look to the right front. (Figure 68)

图 68/Figure 68

动作六：左脚跟向左后蹬转，屈右膝成右弓步，同时，身体向右后拧转，两手环握杖，右手向下，左手向上成立圆转杖约 180° 按压在肩上，杖不离肩；目视右后方。（图 69 正面、图 69 侧面）

Movement 6: Turn your left heel to the left rear and bend your right knee into a right-weighted bow stance. At the same time, twist your body to the right rear. With the right hand upward and left one downward, your hands hold the staff in a ring and turn it about 180 degrees in a vertical circle and press it on the shoulder. Eyes look to the right rear. (Figure 69 front, Figure 69 side)

图 69 正面 /Figure 69 front

图 69 侧面 /Figure 69 side

动作七：身体动作保持不变，继续向下松沉重心，左手杖侧按压左肩井穴，稍停；目视右后方。（图 70）

Movement 7: With the position of your body unchanged, continue to lower the weight. Your left hand holds the staff to press the left *Jianjin* acupoint. Pause for a while. Eyes look to the right rear. (Figure 70)

图 70/Figure 70

　　动作八：右弓步动作保持不变，左手环握杖从肩上向上绕过头，向下落于左胸前，右手环握杖向上画弧至杖右侧把端指向右上方；目视右后方。（图 71 正面、图 71 背面）

Movement 8: With the right-weighted bow stance unchanged, your left hand holds the staff in a ring, upward, over the head, and drops it downward to the left chest. Your right hand holds the staff in a ring and draws an upward arc, the right end of the staff pointing upward to the right rear. Eyes look to the right rear. (Figure 71 front, Figure 71 back)

图 71 正面 /Figure 71 front

图 71 背面 /Figure 71 back

　　动作九：右弓步动作保持不变，身体左转，左手环握杖下落于左腰间，右手环握杖由右后上方向左画弧，杖的右手侧把端随身体转动至体前斜上方；目视杖的方向。（图 72）

Movement 9: With the right-weighted bow stance unchanged, turn your body left. Your left hand holds the staff in a ring and lowers it to the left waist, and your right hand holds the staff in a ring and draws an arc from the upper right rear to the left, the right end of the staff pointing to the upper front. Eyes look in the direction of the staff. (Figure 72)

图 72/Figure 72

动作十：动作不停，身体左转，重心左移，左脚掌向外蹍转，左腿屈膝，右脚尖内扣，右腿自然伸展，同时左手滑杖，随之右手滑杖，杖经小腹右侧经腹前向小腹左侧运转，杖与地面平行；目视杖的方向。（图 73）

Movement 10: Without a pause, turn your body to the left. With the weight shifting to the left, turn the ball of your left foot outward, your left leg bent, and turn your right toes inward, your right leg naturally stretched. At the same time, slide your left hand on the staff to the right, and then slide your right hand on the staff to the left, the staff moving from the right side of the abdomen across the front to the left side of the abdomen, parallel to the ground. Eyes look in the direction of the staff. (Figure 73)

动作十一：左脚收回与右脚并拢，两腿屈膝半蹲，杖向上画弧举至头顶上方，变十指尖向上，两手夹持杖；目视杖的方向。（图 74）

Movement 11: Bring your left foot back to stand with your right foot together, both legs bent in a half squat. The staff draws an arc upward to above your head, hands clamping the staff, fingers pointing upward. Eyes look in the direction of the staff. (Figure 74)

图 73/Figure 73

图 74/Figure 74

动作十二：随即两腿伸展成自然站立，杖下落至胸前，向小腹方向摩运，至两臂自然垂落；目视前方。（图 75）

Movement 12: Straighten your legs to stand naturally. Lower the staff to the chest, and rub it to the lower abdomen until your arms naturally hang down. Eyes look ahead. (Figure 75)

图 75/Figure 75

动作十三：同动作一，唯左右相反。（图 76）

Movement 13: Repeat Movement 1, but with left and right reversed. (Figure 76)

动作十四：同动作二，唯左右相反。（图 77）

Movement 14: Repeat Movement 2, but with left and right reversed. (Figure 77)

图 76/Figure 76

图 77/Figure 77

动作十五：同动作三，唯左右相反。（图 78）

Movement 15: Repeat Movement 3, but with left and right reversed. (Figure 78)

动作十六：同动作四，唯左右相反。（图 79）

Movement 16: Repeat Movement 4, but with left and right reversed. (Figure 79)

动作十七：同动作五，唯左右相反。（图 80）

Movement 17: Repeat Movement 5, but with left and right reversed. (Figure 80)

动作十八：同动作六，唯左右相反。（图 81）

Movement 18: Repeat Movement 6, but with left and right reversed. (Figure 81)

图 78/Figure 78

图 79/Figure 79

图 80/Figure 80

图 81/Figure 81

动作十九：同动作七，唯左右相反。（图 82）

Movement 19: Repeat Movement 7, but with left and right reversed. (Figure 82)

动作二十：同动作八，唯左右相反。（图 83）

Movement 20: Repeat Movement 8, but with left and right reversed. (Figure 83)

图 82/Figure 82

图 83/Figure 83

动作二十一：同动作九，唯左右相反。（图 84）

Movement 21: Repeat Movement 9, but with left and right reversed. (Figure 84)

动作二十二：同动作十，唯左右相反。（图 85）

Movement 22: Repeat Movement 10, but with left and right reversed. (Figure 85)

动作二十三：同动作十一，唯左右相反。（图 86）

Movement 23: Repeat Movement 11, but with left and right reversed. (Figure 86)

动作二十四：同动作十二。（图 87）

Movement 24: Repeat Movement 12. (Figure 87)

图 84/Figure 84

图 85/Figure 85

图 86/Figure 86

图 87/Figure 87

本式一左一右为 1 遍，共做 2 遍。

The movements on the left and the movements on the right form a round. Do two rounds.

二、学练要领

II. Key Points

1. 弓步摩运胁肋部时，手腕要配合卷腕、伸腕的动作。

When rubbing the staff on your rib in a bow stance, you should rotate and extend your wrists.

2. 从弓步时，杖摩运腰侧，至站立时，滑杖按摩大椎穴，再到弓步时杖按压肩井穴，两手向外（杖端）、向内（杖中）滑动，要自然流畅，两手环握杖的位置要对称。

As you do when you rub the staff at the waist in a bow stance and massage *Dazhui* acupoint in standing, you should slide your hands outward (to the end of the staff) and inward (to the middle of the staff) naturally and smoothly when you use the staff to press *Jianjing* acupoint in a bow stance. The positions of holding the staff in a ring with both hands should be symmetrical.

3. 做船夫背纤动作时，立圆转杖要以腰的动作带动杖的圆转，使腰部的拧转和腿部蹬伸更加充分，使身体动作和杖的动作形成整体拧转，做到身体和杖的和谐统一。

When you move like a boatman towing a boat, your should use your waist to drive the movement of the staff, twisting your waist and extending your legs to the full, so that your body and the staff move as a whole.

三、功理功用

III. Functions and Effects

1. 左右转头，可以有效地刺激大椎穴，益气壮阳。

Turning your head to the left or right can effectively stimulate *Dazhui* acupoint, benefiting *Qi* and *Yang*.

2. 用杖按压肩井穴，有利于促进全身气血运行，有助于人体祛风散寒。

Pressing *Jianjing* acupoint with the staff is conducive to promoting the circulation of *Qi* and blood in the whole body, helping to dispel wind and cold.

3. 拧腰、伸膝、蹬脚的弓步动作，有效刺激任督二脉、带脉以及足三阴、足三阳诸经脉，加强全身气血运行，强腰固肾，同时又增大了腰椎和髋关节的活动幅度，使腰腿部肌群得到充分牵拉，有利于腰、腿灵活性和柔韧性的完善与提高。

Twisting the waist and extending the leg in a bow stance can effectively stimulate the *Ren* Meridian, *Du* Meridian and Belt Meridian, and three *Yang* and *Yin* meridians of the foot. It strengthens the circulation of *Qi* and blood in the whole body, reinforcing the waist and the kidneys. At the same time it also increases the ranges of motion of the lumbar vertebrae and hip joints so that the muscles of the waist and leg are fully stretched, which is conducive to the improvement of the flexibility of the waist and the leg.

四、适宜症状

IV. Indications

1. 对前列腺炎、月经不调、头疼、中风等症状有辅助康复的作用。

It is an aid to recovery from prostatitis, irregular menstruation, headache or stroke.

2. 有利于颈肩部和腰背部肌肉酸痛的调治。

It can help to alleviate the pain in the neck, waist or back.

第五式　神针定海

Posture 5　*Ruyi* Staff Calms the Sea

一、功法操作

I. Instructions

动作一：接上式，两腿微屈膝，左脚向左侧开步，约与肩宽，脚尖向前，同时，左手环握杖，手心向下，右手腕外旋翻转手心向上托杖；目视右手方向。（图 88）

Movement 1: Continuing from the end of the previous posture, bend your knees slightly. Take a step to the left with your left foot, about shoulder-width apart, with the toes pointing forward. At the same time, your left hand holds the staff in a ring, palm facing downward; and with the wrist rotating outwardly, your right hand holds the staff up, palm facing up. Eyes look in the direction of your right hand. (Figure 88)

图 88/Figure 88

动作二：两脚不动，重心移至两腿中间，两膝微屈，同时两手夹持杖从身体右侧移动到身体左侧，杖在腹前移动与地面平行；目视左侧。（图 89）

Movement 2: With the position of your two feet unchanged, shift the weight to be evenly distributed across your feet, knees slightly bent. At the same time, your hands clamp the staff and move it from the right side of your body to the left. When the staff moves in front of your abdomen, it is parallel to the ground. Eyes look to the left. (Figure 89)

动作三：随即两腿自然伸展，杖由腹前从左侧向上画立圆，举至头上与地面平行；目随杖走。（图 90）

Movement 3: Then straighten your legs naturally. The staff draws upward in a vertical circle from the left front of your abdomen. When the staff is above your head, it is parallel to the ground. Eyes follow the staff. (Figure 90)

图 89/Figure 89

图 90/Figure 90

动作四：两腿屈膝半蹲，杖向身体右侧弧形下落，约与腰同高；目随杖走。（图 91）

Movement 4: With your legs bent in a half squat, the staff falls to the right side of your body in an arc, about the same height as your waist. Eyes follow the staff. (Figure 91)

动作五：两腿自然站立，身体右转，左手外旋手心向上握杖，旋杖于胸前，右手随杖运行下落于右小腹前，手心向上，杖左手端在上，右手端在下，在身体右侧立杖与地面夹角约为 45°；目视杖的方向。（图 92）

Movement 5: Straighten your legs naturally. With your body turning right, rotate your left hand holding the staff outward to your chest, palm up; drop your right hand to your right abdomen, palm up. At the end of the trajectory, the end of the staff close to your left hand is on top, and the end close to your right hand is on the bottom. The angle between the staff and the ground on the right side of your body is about 45 degrees. Eyes look in the direction of the staff. (Figure 92)

图 91/Figure 91

图 92/Figure 92

动作六：身体左转约 180°，左脚外展约 90°，右脚跟向后蹬转成左弓步，两手变夹持杖立杖画平圆从右向左随身体左转运行于体前。（图 93 正面、图 93 侧面）

Movement 6: With your body turning left about 180 degrees, turn your left foot outward about 90 degrees and turn your right heel backward to form a left-weighted bow stance. Your hands clamp the staff and draw a horizontal circle from right to left as your body turns left, until the staff reaches the front of your body. (Figure 93 front, Figure 93 side)

图 93 正面 /Figure 93 front

图 93 侧面 /Figure 93 side

动作七：右脚上步，与左脚平行，约与肩同宽，两腿屈膝半蹲，同时，左手卷旋环握，杖端向下画弧至与胸同高，右手稍向左手杖端滑动，杖端由下向上画圆弧，至约与地面平行；目视杖的方向。（图 94 正面、图 94 侧面）

Movement 7: Take a step forward with your right foot, parallel to your left foot, about shoulder-width apart. Bend your knees in a half squat. At the same time, rotate your left hand to hold the staff in a ring, the end of the staff drawing an arc downward to about chest height. Slide your right hand slightly towards the left end of the staff, drawing an arc upward from below until it is approximately parallel to the ground. Eyes look in the direction of the staff. (Figure 94 front, Figure 94 side)

图 94 正面 /Figure 94 front

图 94 侧面 /Figure 94 side

动作八：动作不停，左手握杖端继续向下画弧至与腰同高，右手握杖端继续向上画弧至稍高于肩，杖在体前与地面垂直；目视杖的方向。（图 95）

Movement 8: Without a pause, the end of the staff close to your left hand continues to draw an arc downward to about waist height, while the end of the staff close to your right hand continues to draw an arc upward to slightly above the shoulder. The staff is vertical to the ground in front of your body. Eyes look in the direction of the staff. (Figure 95)

动作九：身体动作保持不变，右手环握杖从上向下滑落杖触及左手；目视前方。（图 96）

Movement 9: With the position of your body unchanged, slide your right hand holding the staff in a ring downward from above until it touches your left hand. Eyes look ahead. (Figure 96)

图 95/Figure 95

图 96/Figure 96

动作十：两腿自然站立，同时，两手下落至腹前分开，两臂经体侧伸直，右手持杖，右手杖端向下，杖贴于右臂后侧，左手自然落于体侧；目视前方。（图 97）

Movement 10: Straighten your legs naturally. At the same time, lower your hands to the front of your abodomen, and separate them to both sides of your body, straightened. Hold the staff with your right hand, the end of the staff close to your right hand pointing downwards, the staff attached to the back of your right arm. Your left hand naturally falls at the left side of your body. Eyes look ahead. (Figure 97)

动作十一：身体动作保持不变，左臂外旋向体左前约 45° 上举，手心向上，与头同高；目视掌的方向。（图 98 正面、图 98 侧面）

Movement 11: With the position of your body unchanged, lift

your outward-rotating left arm up about 45 degrees to the left front of your body, palm facing up at the same height as your head. Eyes look in the direction of the palm. (Figure 98 front, Figure 98 side)

图 97/Figure 97

图 98 正面 /Figure 98 front

图 98 侧面 /Figure 98 side

动作十二：两腿微屈膝，左臂屈肘，手掌心向下，经面前从上向下按掌至腹前；目视前方。（图 99）

Movement 12: With your knees slightly bent, bend your left elbow, palm facing downward. Press your left palm downward from above to the front of the abdomen. Eyes look ahead. (Figure 99).

动作十三：右脚向后退一步，身体右转约 90°，左脚尖内扣，两脚尖向前，约与肩宽，两腿微屈膝，同时，左手手心向上接杖环握至杖左侧三分之一处，右手手心向下滑杖至杖右侧三分之一处；目视前下方。（图 100）

Movement 13: Take a step backward with your right foot, your body turning about 90 degrees to the right. With your left toes turning inward, the toes of your feet point forward, about shoulder-width apart. Bend your knees slightly. At the same time, hold the staff in a ring with your left hand at one third of the length from its left end, and slide your right hand on the staff to one third of the length from its right end. Eyes look downward to the front. (Figure 100)

图 99/Figure 99

图 100/Figure 100

动作十四：上体保持中正，重心右移，右手夹持杖，手心向下，左手手心向上托杖；杖由身体左侧向右侧平移；目视右手方向。（图 101）

Movement 14: With your upper body upright, shift the weight to the right. Clamp the staff with your right hand, palm down. Hold the staff up with your left hand, palm up. Move the staff horizontally from the left side of your body to the right side. Eyes look in the direction of your left hand. (Figure 101)

图 101/Figure 101

动作十五：同动作三，唯左右相反。（图 102）

Movement 15: Repeat Movement 3, but with left and right reversed. (Figure 102)

动作十六：同动作四，唯左右相反。（图 103）

Movement 16: Repeat Movement 4, but with left and right reversed. (Figure 103)

动作十七：同动作五，唯左右相反。（图 104）

Movement 17: Repeat Movement 5, but with left and right reversed. (Figure 104)

动作十八：同动作六，唯左右相反。（图 105）

Movement 18: Repeat Movement 6, but with left and right reversed. (Figure 105)

图 102/Figure 102

图 103/Figure 103

图 104/Figure 104

图 105/Figure 105

动作十九：同动作七，唯左右相反。（图 106）

Movement 19: Repeat Movement 7, but with left and right reversed. (Figure 106)

动作二十：同动作八，唯左右相反。（107）

Movement 20: Repeat Movement 8, but with left and right reversed. (Figure 107)

图 106/Figure 106

图 107/Figure 107

动作二十一：同动作九，唯左右相反。（图 108）

Movement 21: Repeat Movement 9, but with left and right reversed. (Figure 108)

动作二十二：同动作十，唯左右相反。（图 109）

Movement 22: Repeat Movement 10, but with left and right reversed. (Figure 109)

动作二十三：同动作十一，唯左右相反。（图 110）

Movement 23: Repeat Movement 11, but with left and right reversed. (Figure 110)

动作二十四：同动作十二，唯左右相反。（图 111）

Movement 24: Repeat Movement 12, but with left and right reversed. (Figure 111)

图 108/Figure 108

图 109/Figure 109

图 110/Figure 110

图 111/Figure 111

本式一左一右为 1 遍，共做 2 遍。

The movements on the left and the movements on the right form a round. Do two rounds.

二、学练要领

II. Key Points

1. 完整动作练习时，两手夹持杖、环握杖、托杖、旋杖、卷杖、滑杖要自然流畅。

When you practice the movements, your hands should clamp the staff, hold the staff in a ring, lift the staff, rotate the staff, curl the staff and slide on the staff naturally and smoothly.

2. 旋杖、卷杖、滑杖等基本动作，可以作为太极导引杖的基本功单独进行练习。

The basic movements such as rotating the staff, curling the staff, and sliding your hand on the staff can be practiced as fundamental skills for Taiji Daoyinzhang separately.

3. 呼吸与动作配合，刚刚学练时建议采用自然呼吸，动作熟练后，应遵循起吸落呼的呼吸规律，随着对技术要领的深入、细致的掌握，呼吸会逐渐变得细、匀、深、长，再过渡到腹式呼吸。

Coordinate breathing with movements. It is recommended to use natural breathing when you practice it at the initial stage. After becoming skilled in the movements, your should inhale when rising and exhale when falling. As your skills advance, your breathing will gradually become quiet, even, deep and long, and then transition to abdominal breathing.

4. 手臂上举、下按时，意念纳天地之精华，归入丹田，稍停。

When lifting and pressing your arm, imagine absorbing the essence of nature into *Dantian*. Pause for a while.

三、功理功用

III. Functions and Effects

1. 手腕的卷旋、圆转运动，可以刺激手三阴经和手三阳经原穴，充分抻拉肺经、心经和心包经，起到宣发肺气、调畅气机的作用。

Wrist rotation can stimulate the acupoints of the three *Yin* and *Yang* meridians of the hand, fully stretching the Lung Meridian, Heart Meridian, and Pericardium Meridian, to ventilate the lung *Qi* and regulate *Qi* circulation.

2. 下肢弓步、马步、偏马步的活桩变化，促进下肢气血的运行。

The changes of bow stance, horse-riding stance and right/left-weighted horse-riding stance can promote the flow of *Qi* and blood in the lower limbs.

3. 以杖导引行气，意气相合，捧天地泰和之气，由百会入丹田，可培补元气，提高练功效果。

Using the staff to guide the flow of *Qi*, combining your mind and *Qi*, and absorbing the essence of nature into *Dantian* from *Baihui* acupoint, can cultivate and replenish the vital energy and improve the practice effect.

四、适宜症状

IV. Indications

1. 预防感冒，缓解咳喘症状。

It can prevent colds and relieve symptoms of coughing and wheezing.

2. 预防和缓解情绪抑郁、脾气急躁、易怒等症状，对两胁肋部疼痛有辅助康复的作用。

It can prevent and relieve symptoms of emotional depression, short-temperedness, irritability, and assist in the rehabilitation of pain in the ribs.

3. 腕关节的卷旋有利于缓解腕管综合征（鼠标手）的症状。

Wrist rotation is beneficial to relieving the symptoms of carpal tunnel syndrome (mouse hand).

第六式　金龙绞尾

Posture 6　Dragon Wags Tail

一、功法操作

I. Instructions

动作一：接上式，右脚内扣，身体左转约 45°，右手手心向下，小指端向前接杖并环握杖；目视前下方。（图 112）

Movement 1: Continuing from the end of the previous posture, with your right foot turned inward, turn your body about 45 degrees to the left. With the little finger forward, hold the staff in a ring with your right hand, palm down. Eyes look to the lower front. (Figure 112)

动作二：动作不停，左脚向左后约 45°退步，引导杖端向右前方约 45°前伸，左手滑杖至杖左手端；目视前下方。（图 113）

Movement 2: Without a pause, step backward with your left foot at an angle of about 45 degrees to the left, guide the end of the staff forward to the right at an angle of about 45 degrees, slide your left hand on the staff to its left end. Eyes look to the lower front. (Figure 113)

动作三：动作不停，身体左转约 180°，左脚掌向外碾转，右脚掌向内碾，屈膝成左弓步；同时杖右手端向上、向前、向下画立圆至与肩同高，左手握杖置于右腋下；目视杖的方向。（图 114 正面、图 114 侧面）

Movement 3: Without a pause, turn your body to the left by about 180 degrees. Pivot the ball of your left foot outward and the ball of your right foot inward, and bend the knees into a left-weighted bow stance. At the same time, the end of the staff close to your right hand draws a vertical circle upward, forward, and downward to a height level with your shoulder, while your left hand holding the staff under your right armpit. Eyes look in the direction of the staff. (Figure 114 front, Figure 114 side)

图 112/Figure 112

图 113/Figure 113

图 114 正面 /Figure 114 front

图 114 侧面 /Figure 114 side

动作四：重心后坐，右腿屈膝，左腿自然伸展，同时，左掌向前滑杖至左手杖端环握杖，稍高于肩，右掌向后滑杖于右腰间环握杖；目视前方。（图 115 正面、图 115 侧面）

Movement 4: With the weight shifting backward, bend your right knee, and straighten your left leg naturally. At the same time, slide your left hand forward on the staff to hold its left end in a ring, slightly higher than your left shoulder. Slide your right hand backward on the staff to hold it in a ring at your right waist. Eyes look ahead. (Figure 115 front, Figure 115 side)

图 115 正面 /Figure 115 front

图 115 侧面 /Figure 115 side

动作五：杖的动作保持不变，左脚经右脚内侧向后退步，与右腿成交叉步，两膝微屈；目视前方。（图 116 正面、图 116 侧面）

Movement 5: With the position of the staff unchanged, step backward with your left foot inside your right foot to form a cross stance with your right leg, knees slightly bent. Eyes look ahead. (Figure 116 front, Figure 116 side)

图 116 正面 /Figure 116 front

图 116 侧面 /Figure 116 side

动作六：身体右转约 45°，成高歇步，左膝抵压右小腿承山穴，稍停；目视右前方。（图 117 正面、图 117 背面）

Movement 6: Turn your body to the right by about 45 degrees to form a high rest stance, your left knee pressing against *Chengshan*

图 117 正面 /Figure 117 front

图 117 背面 /Figure 117 back

acupoint on your right calf. Pause for a while. Eyes look to the right front. (Figure 117 front, Figure 117 back)

动作七：两腿屈膝下蹲成歇步，左手向身体右斜下方插杖，杖端贴近地面，左掌向上托杖，右手杖端触地，掌心向下环握杖；目视杖端。（图 118 正面、图 118 背面）

Movement 7: Bend your knees into a rest stance. Thrust the staff downward to the right with your left hand, the left end of the staff close to the ground. Hold the staff up with your left hand, the right end of the staff touching the ground, palm down. Eyes look at the right end of the staff. (Figure 118 front, Figure 118 back)

图 118 正面 /Figure 118 front

图 118 背面 /Figure 118 back

动作八：歇步动作保持不变，左掌向前、向上，内旋转掌心向下绞杖，向下压杖，两掌心均向下夹持杖；目视杖右手端方向。（图 119）

Movement 8: With your rest stance unchanged, stir with the staff, your left hand moving forward, upward, and rotating inward, palm down, and press the staff downward. Clamp the staff with your hands, palms downward. Eyes look at the right end of the staff. (Figure 119)

动作九：两腿自然站立，左脚向左侧开一步，脚尖向前，同时，左手环握杖向身体左侧水平引杖，右手夹持杖向右端滑杖；目视杖的方向。（图 120）

Movement 9: Straighten your legs naturally. Take a step to the left with your left foot, toes forward. At the same time, hold the staff in a ring with your left hand and swing it horizontally to the left side of the body. Clamp the staff with your right hand and slide it right on the staff. Eyes look in the direction of the staff. (Figure 120)

图 119/Figure 119

图 120/Figure 120

动作十：右脚收回，两脚并步自然站立，左手向右滑杖至杖左手端约 1/3 处，两手约与肩同宽，环握杖自然垂落于体前；目视前方。（图 121）

Movement 10: Bring your right foot back and stand naturally with both feet together. Slide your left hand on the staff to about one third of the length close to its left end. Hold the staff in a ring with your hands and hang it in front of your body, about shoulder-width apart. Eyes look ahead. (Figure 121)

动作十一：同动作二，唯左右相反。（图 122）

Movement 11: Repeat Movement 2, but with left and right reversed. (Figure 122)

图 121/Figure 121

图 122/Figure 122

动作十二：同动作三，唯左右相反。（图 123 正面、图 123 侧面）

Movement 12: Repeat Movement 3, but with left and right reversed. (Figure 123 front, Figure 123 side)

图 123 正面 /Figure 123 front

图 123 侧面 /Figure 123 side

动作十三：同动作四，唯左右相反。（图 124 正面、图 124 侧面）

Movement 13: Repeat Movement 4, but with left and right reversed. (Figure 124 front, Figure 124 side)

图 124 正面 /Figure 124 front

图 124 侧面 /Figure 124 side

动作十四：同动作五，唯左右相反。（图 125）

Movement 14: Repeat Movement 5, but with left and right reversed. (Figure 125)

动作十五：同动作六，唯左右相反。（图 126 正面、图 126 背面）

图 125/Figure 125

图 126 正面 /Figure 126 front

图 126 背面 /Figure 126 back

Movement 15: Repeat Movement 6, but with left and right reversed. (Figure 126 front, Figure 126 back)

动作十六：同动作七，唯左右相反。（图 127 正面、图 127 背面）

Movement 16: Repeat Movement 7, but with left and right reversed. (Figure 127 front, Figure 127 back)

图 127 正面 /Figure 127 front

图 127 背面 /Figure 127 back

动作十七：同动作八，唯左右相反。（图 128）

Movement 17: Repeat Movement 8, but with left and right reversed. (Figure 128)

动作十八：同动作九，唯左右相反。（图 129）

Movement 18: Repeat Movement 9, but with left and right reversed. (Figure 129)

动作十九：同动作十，唯左右相反。（图 130）

Movement 19: Repeat Movement 10, but with left and right reversed. (Figure 130)

图 128/Figure 128

图 129/Figure 129

图 130/Figure 130

本式一左一右为 1 遍，共做 2 遍。

The movements on the left and the movements on the right form around. Do two rounds.

二、学练要领

II. Key Points

1. 练习金龙绞尾时，要注意身体时刻保持平衡状态，杖向前引伸时，腿向后退步，杖由下向上立圆转动，脚下踝转向下松沉变弓步。练习时要充分体现有前必有后、有上必有下的对拔平衡的太极阴阳关系。

When practicing Dragon Wags Tail, always keep your body in balance. When you extend the staff forward, your opposite leg should take a step backward. When you draw a vertical circle with the staff upward, you should pivot the balls of your feet and sink into a bow stance. In practice, it is essential to fully embody the balanced forward-backward and upward-downward relationships.

2. 立圆转动杖时，肩、肘、手要放松，自然伸展手臂。

When drawing a vertical circle with the staff, you should relax your shoulders, elbows, and hands, and extend your arms naturally.

3. 两手相向滑杖时，要沉肩、垂肘，手腕放松，做到手不离杖，杖不离身。

When sliding your hands on the staff towards each other, you should relax your shoulders and wrists, and drop your elbows. Keep your hands on the staff, and staff on your body.

4. 动作与呼吸相配合，绞杖时手腕外旋，配合吸气，手腕内旋两手向下压杖时，配合呼气；起身、开步时配合吸气，两脚并步时，配合呼气。

Coordinate breathing with movements. When stirring with the staff, you should rotate your left wrist outward coupled with inhalation, and when pressing the staff downward with both hands, you should rotate your left wrist inward coupled with exhalation. When straightening your legs and take a step to the left with your left foot, inhale, and when bringing your right foot back to stand with both feet together, exhale.

5. 中老年人及高血压、冠心病患者练习者，可选择高歇步。随着中老年人身体素质的逐渐增强，可自由选择高、低歇步。

Middle-aged and elderly practitioners, as well as those with hypertension and coronary heart disease, can choose a high rest stance. As their physical fitness gradually improves, they can choose between high rest stance and low rest stance.

三、功理功用
III. Functions and Effects

1. 练习高歇步抵压承山穴，可以振奋足太阳膀胱经的阳气，促进肾水代谢，排出人体湿气。

Pressing against *Chengshan* acupoint in a high rest stance can invigorate the *Yang Qi* of Bladder Meridian of Foot-*Taiyang* and promote the metabolism of kidney fluid to expel moisture from human body.

2. 以腰为轴左右转体，有节奏地刺激带脉，有利于全身经脉之气的调畅。

Turning your body around the waist to the left and right stimulates the Belt Meridian in a rhythmic manner, which is beneficial for the regulation of *Qi* flow throughout the entire body.

3. 低歇步可提高下肢柔韧性，加强下肢肌肉的力量，提高平衡能力。

A low rest stance can improve lower limb flexibility, strengthen lower limb muscles and improve balance.

四、适宜症状
IV. Indications

1. 可以预防和缓解腓肠肌痉挛、腰背痛等症状。

It can prevent and relieve gastrocnemius muscle spasm and low back pain.

2. 对便秘、脱肛、痔疮有辅助康复的作用。

It is an aid to recovery from constipation, prolapse and hemorrhoids.

第七式　探海寻宝

Posture 7　Search for Treasure in the Sea

一、功法操作

I. Instructions

动作一：接上式，左脚侧开一步，两脚尖向前，约与肩宽，自然站立，同时，两手环握杖向体前平举，杖至与肩同高，两手与肩同宽；目视前方。（图 131）

Movement 1: Continuing from the end of the previous posture, take a step to the left with your left foot, about shoulder-width apart, with the toes pointing forward. At the same time, hold the staff in a ring with your hands and lift it horizontally in front of your body until the staff is at the same height as your shoulders, hands shoulder-width

图 131/Figure 131

apart. Eyes look ahead. (Figure 131)

动作二：身体保持自然站立，沉肩、屈肘、两手环握杖坐腕手心向前，杖收回于胸前；目视前方。（图 132）

Movement 2: Stand naturally, shoulders relaxed, elbows bent. With both hands holding the staff in a ring, settle your wrists, palms facing forward. Bring the staff back to the chest. Eyes look ahead. (Figure 132)

动作三：身体动作保持不变，两手环握杖旋腕手心向内，卷杖于两乳下；目视前方。（图 133）

Movement 3: With the position of your body unchanged, hold the staff in a ring with your hands and rotate your wrists, palms inward, rolling the staff to under the breasts. Eyes look ahead. (Figure 133)

图 132/Figure 132

图 133/Figure 133

动作四：两手环握杖从胸前沿腹部向下摩运，至两臂自然伸展；目视前方。（图 134）

Movement 4: Hold the staff in a ring with your hands and rub it downward from the chest to the abdomen until your arms naturally extend. Eyes look ahead. (Figure 134)

动作五：上体前屈，杖继续摩运至两脚尖前，双手轻触地面，两腿自然伸展；目随杖走。（图 135）

Movement 5: With your upper body bent forward, rub the staff further to the toes of your feet, your hands touching the ground, your legs naturally straightened. Eyes follow the staff. (Figure 135)

图 134/Figure 134

图 135/Figure 135

动作六：两腿微屈膝，两手环握杖向左平移；目视杖的方向。（图 136）

Movement 6: With your knees slightly bent, hold the staff in a ring with your hands and move it horizontally to the left. Eyes look in the direction of the staff. (Figure 136)

动作七：上体左转，与地面平行，两腿自然伸展，向左转头，弧形向上举杖，右手向左上方摆起至左腋旁，左手环握杖上举至杖与地面垂直，左臂自然伸展；目视杖的左手上端。（图 137 正面、图 137 侧面）

Movement 7: Turn your upper body to the left, parallel to the ground, and straighten your legs naturally. With your head turning to the left, lift the staff upward in an arc. Swing your right hand to the upper left to your left armpit, and lift the staff with your left hand until the staff is vertical to the ground, your left arm naturally extended. Eyes look at the end of the staff close to your left hand. (Figure 137 front, Figure 137 side)

图 136/Figure 136

图 137 正面 /Figure 137 front

图 137 侧面 /Figure 137 side

动作八：身体右转成体前屈，放松，两膝微屈，微弓背，杖弧形垂落于脚尖前，手臂自然伸展，双手轻触地面；目随杖走。（图 138）

Movement 8: Turn the body to the right and bend forward. With your body relaxed, bend your knees slightly and arch your back slightly. Drop the staff in an arc to the toes of your feet, arms naturally extended, hands lightly touching the ground. Eyes follow the staff. (Figure 138)

图 138/Figure 138

动作九：两膝自然伸展，同时，塌腰、抬头、吸气，稍停；目视前方。（图 139 正面、图 139 侧面）

Movement 9: Straighten your legs naturally. At the same time, sink your waist, lift your head, inhale. Pause for a while. Eyes look ahead. (Figure 139 front, Figure 139 side)

动作十：身体放松，呼气，两手环握卷杖，杖沿两腿前向上摩运至两乳下；目视前方。（图 140）

Movement 10: Relax your body and exhale. Hold the staff in a ring with your hands and rub it along the legs upward to under the breasts. Eyes look ahead. (Figure 140)

动作十一：左脚收回成并步站立，两手环握杖，手腕放松，向下经腹部摩运至两臂自然伸展；目视前方（图 141）

Movement 11: Bring your left foot back and stand with both feet together. With your wrists relaxed, hold the staff in a ring with your hands and rub it down along the abdomen until your arms naturally extend. Eyes look ahead. (Figure 141)

图 139 正面 /Figure 139 front

图 139 侧面 /Figure 139 side

图 140/Figure 140

图 141/Figure 141

动作十二：同动作一，唯左右相反。（图 142）

Movement 12: Repeat Movement 1, but with left and right reversed. (Figure 142)

动作十三：同动作二。（图 143）

Movement 13: Repeat Movement 2. (Figure 143)

动作十四：同动作三。（图 144）

Movement 14: Repeat Movement 3. (Figure 144)

图 142/Figure 142

图 143/Figure 143

图 144/Figure 144

动作十五：同动作四。（图 145）

Movement 15: Repeat Movement 4. (Figure 145)

动作十六：同动作五。（图 146）

Movement 16: Repeat Movement 5. (Figure 146)

图 145/Figure 145

图 146/Figure 146

动作十七：同动作六，唯左右相反。（图 147）

Movement 17: Repeat Movement 6, but with left and right reversed. (Figure 147)

图 147/Figure 147

动作十八：同动作七，唯左右相反。（图 148 正面、图 148 侧面）

Movement 18: Repeat Movement 7, but with left and right reversed. (Figure 148 front, Figure 148 side)

图 148 正面 /Figure 148 front

图 148 侧面 /Figure 148 side

动作十九：同动作八，唯左右相反。（图 149）

Movement 19: Repeat Movement 8, but with left and right reversed. (Figure 149)

图 149/Figure 149

动作二十：同动作九。（图 150 正面、图 150 侧面）

Movement 20: Repeat Movement 9. (Figure 150 front, Figure 150 side)

动作二十一：同动作十。（图 151）

Movement 21: Repeat Movement 10. (Figure 151)

动作二十二：同动作十一，唯左右相反。（图 152）

Movement 22: Repeat Movement 11, but with left and right reversed. (Figure 152)

图 150 正面 /Figure 150 front

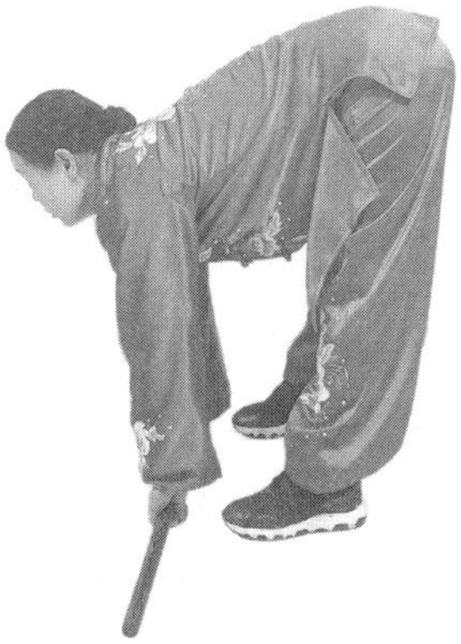

图 150 侧面 /Figure 150 side

图 151/Figure 151

图 152/Figure 152

本式一左一右为 1 遍，共做 2 遍。

The movements on the left and the movements on the right form a round. Do two rounds.

二、学练要领

II. Key Points

1. 练习探海寻宝动作时，要时刻意念以杖导引，平举杖、收回杖、落杖摩运，要以杖为主导，充分感受杖的自然流畅。

When practicing Search for Treasure in the Sea, focus your mind on the staff. When you lift the staff horizontally, bring it back, or lower it to rub, you should take the staff as dominant, and fully feel the smooth movement of the staff.

2. 身体前屈向左、右转体举杖时，转头要充分，上体要水平。

When bending forward and turning your body to lift the staff to the left or right, your should turn your head as far as possible, and ensure your upper body is level.

3. 初学者以及中老年人做体前屈时，俯身要适度，以不憋气或胸腹没有压迫感为宜，保持呼吸顺畅。

Beginners, middle-aged or elderly people should bend forward moderately so as not to feel choked or oppressive in their chest and abdomen. Keep their breathing smooth.

三、功理功用

III. Functions and Effects

1. 本式动作转体、转头、体前屈、抬头、塌腰等，可以有效地刺激任脉、督脉和带脉，加强全身气血运行，起到壮阳益气，宁心安神的作用。

Turning your body or head, bending your body forward, lifting your head, and sinking your waist can effectively stimulate *Ren*

Meridian, *Du* Meridian and Belt Meridian and promote the circulation of *Qi* and blood to strengthen *Yang*, replenish *Qi*, and calm the heart and nerves.

2. 躯体的前俯，侧屈扭转，可以充分锻炼腰背肌，有利于腰部运动不适的预防与调治。

The forward bending and lateral twisting of the body can fully exercise the back muscles, which is beneficial to the prevention and treatment of discomfort in lower back.

3. 在前俯到位后拧转颈项，不仅可以加大牵拉腰背肌的力量，而且有利于对颈部背部运动不适的预防与调治。

Twisting the neck after bending you body forward can not only increase the strength of pulling back muscles, but also help to prevent and treat discomfort in neck or back.

四、适宜症状
IV. Indications

1. 对前列腺炎、月经不调、头疼、中风等症状有辅助康复的作用。

It is an aid to recovery from prostatitis, irregular menstruation, headache and stroke.

2. 有利于肩肘、手部、颈部和腰背部肌肉酸痛的调治。

It is conducive to the treatment of muscle soreness in the shoulders, elbows, hands, neck, and lower back.

第八式　气归丹田

Posture 8　*Qi* Returns to *Dantian*

一、功法操作

I. Instructions

动作一：接上式，身体动作保持不变，左手变掌，掌心向下贴杖，杖平行于地面；目视前方。（图 153）

Movement 1: Continuing from the end of the previous posture, with the position of your body unchanged, open your left hand into a palm, facing down, pressed against the staff, the staff parallel to the ground. Eyes look ahead. (Figure 153)

图 153/Figure 153

动作二：身体动作保持不变，左手贴杖向外旋腕，变掌心向上夹持杖，杖平行于地面；目视前方。（图 154）

Movement 2: With the position of your body unchanged, rotate your left hand outward on the staff and clamp it, palm up, the staff parallel to the ground. Eyes look ahead. (Figure 154)

动作三：杖的左手端贴于左臂内侧，右手端下落，杖垂直地面，两臂自然垂于身体两侧，左脚侧开一步，约与肩同宽，两脚尖向前，自然站立；目视前方。（图 155）

Movement 3: With the end of the staff close to your left hand against the inside of your left arm, lower the end close to your right hand, the staff vertical to the ground, arms hanging naturally on both sides of your body. Take a step with your left foot about shoulder-width apart, and stand naturally with the toes of your feet pointing forward. Eyes look ahead. (Figure 155)

图 154/Figure 154

图 155/Figure 155

动作四：身体动作保持不变，两臂内旋，两手分别向两侧摆起，手臂与身体的角度约 45°；目视前方。（图 156）

Movement 4: With the position of your body unchanged, rotate your arms internally, swinging your hands to the sides of your body, each at an angle of about 45 degrees to the body. Eyes look ahead. (Figure 156)

动作五：上动不停，两腿屈膝，同时，两臂外旋，两掌合抱于小腹前，掌心向内，指尖相对，约距 10 厘米，杖垂直地面；目视前方，稍停。（图 157）

Movement 5: Without a pause, bend your knees. At the same time, rotate your arms outward, bringing your palms close to each other in front of the lower abdomen about 10 centimetres apart, palms facing inward, fingertips pointing to each other, the staff vertical to the ground. Eyes look ahead. Pause for a while. (Figure 157)

图 156/Figure 156

图 157/Figure 157

动作六：两腿自然站立，两手向肚脐下收拢，随即两臂自然分开垂于体侧；目视前方。（图 158）

Movement 6: Straighten your legs naturally and bring your hands together under the navel. Then separate your arms and let them hang naturally on both sides of your body. Eyes look ahead. (Figure 158)

图 158/Figure 158

动作四、动作五、动作六共做 3 遍。

Repeat Movements 4, 5, and 6 for three times.

二、学练要领

II. Key Points

1. 左手从掌心向下环握杖到旋腕掌心向上夹持杖，整个过程要自然流畅。

The whole process should be natural and smooth, from holding the staff in a ring with your left hand, palm down, to rotating your left wrist and clamping the staff with your left hand, palm up.

2. 杖端下落时，要柔和匀速，两手侧起、合抱、收拢、下落时，杖均垂直于地面，杖端不要碰地。

When the end of the staff falls, it should be soft and even. When you swing your hands sideways, bring them together, and lower them, make sure that the staff is vertical to the ground, and the end of the staff should not touch the ground.

三、功理功用

III. Functions and Effects

以意引气归丹田，有助于壮中气、补元气，滋养脏腑，平调阴阳。

Use your mind to direct *Qi* to *Dantian* can help strengthen the Middle *Qi*, replenish vital energy, nourish the organs, and balance *Yin* and *Yang*.

四、适宜症状

IV. Indications

缓解内心焦虑、精神紧张等症状。

It can relieve inner anxiety and mental stress.

收　势

Closing

一、功法操作

I. Instructions

接上式，左脚收回自然站立；目视前方，稍停。（图 159）

Continuing from the end of the previous posture, bring your left foot back and stand naturally with both feet together. Eyes look ahead. Pause for a while. (Figure 159)

图 159/Figure 159

二、学练要领

II. Key Points

站立时两肩松沉，身体中正，自然放松，意念由动复静，巩固丹田元气，使身心调节到最佳的放松和平衡状态。

Stand with relaxed shoulders, a upright body and a peaceful mind. Reinforce your *Qi* in *Dantian*, adjusting your body and mind to the best state of relaxation and balance.

三、适宜症状

III. Indications

顺利完成机体和系统由气功状态向日常生活状态的过渡，避免因收功不及时带来的身心不适。

A successful transition from a *Qigong* state to a daily life state can avoid the discomfort that may arise from not properly closing the practice.

太极导引杖的呼吸要求

Breathing Requirements

太极导引杖的呼吸与动作配合的总体规律是起吸落呼、开吸合呼。呼吸的形式主要是自然呼吸和腹式呼吸。自然呼吸是不加意念控制的自由呼吸。腹式呼吸是有意识地将呼吸与肢体动作协调配合，使呼吸更加细、匀、深、长。习练者应根据自身动作的熟练程度，先采用自然呼吸，再慢慢过渡到腹式呼吸，两者结合运用，最终达到“导气令和”的健身目的。

The overall requirement for breathing and movement coordination in Taiji Daoyinzhang is to inhale while rising or opening and exhale while falling or closing. The main forms of breathing are natural and abdominal. Natural breathing is free without mind control. Abdominal breathing is to coordinate breathing and body movements with the mind, making breathing more quiet, even, deep and long. Practitioners should gradually transition from natural breathing to abdominal breathing as they become more proficient in movements. The combination of natural breathing and abdominal breathing can help achieve the fitness goal of “guiding the flow of *Qi* to achieve harmony”.

学习建议

Learning Tips

1. 清楚动作的路线和节点。

Be clear about the route and transitional movements.

2. 杖是身体的一部分，做到手不离杖，杖不离身，身械协调。

The staff is an extension of your body. Keep your hands on the staff, and staff on your body. Coordinate the movements of your body and the staff.

3. 站桩筑基，正形调气，感悟动作的要求、要领和呼吸方法。

Standing meditation is the foundation. Rectify postures, adjust breathing, experience and understand the requirements, essentials, and breathing methods in practice.

4. 了解和掌握动作所涉及的脏腑经络和穴位。

Understand and master the internal organs, meridians and acupoints involved in the movements.

5. 整套动作练习时，要以杖导引，身心放松，意境优美，意气相随。

When practicing the entire set of movements, focus your mind on the staff and relax your body and mind, with a beautiful artistic conception. Mind and *Qi* are unified.

6. 技礼并重，体悟明理。

Emphasize both skills and etiquette, and grasp the principles through personal exercise.